THE WAITING MISSIONARY

The Waiting Missionary

Written by David E. Fessenden

Illustrated by Brenda Wintermyer (Step One Design)

The Waiting Missionary is a story in the *Missionary—That's Me!* series

CHRISTIAN PUBLICATIONS / Camp Hill, Pennsylvania

Faithful, biblical publishing since 1883

For Rev. Timothy Poferl,
the *real* Pastor Luis

Christian Publications
3825 Hartzdale Drive, Camp Hill, PA 17011

ISBN: 0-87509-561-5
Printed in the United States of America

95 96 97 98 99 5 4 3 2 1

My sister Jasmine and I sat in the front pew at church, waiting for the children's sermon by Pastor Luis. He's our new assistant pastor and we really like his sermons. Sometimes he tells a story; sometimes he brings something for us to look at. Today he came in wearing a funny hat.

"Boys and girls, this is called a pith helmet," he said. "Does this remind you of anyone with a special job?"

"A big game hunter in Africa," Sally said.

"An explorer," Randy said.

"I know!" my sister said. "A missionary!"

"That's right!" said Pastor Luis. "A pith helmet was what some missionaries used to wear to protect themselves from the hot sun or falling rocks. Nowadays, they usually wear the same kind of clothes that you and I do. But you'll find out all about that, because tonight we'll have a real, live missionary speak to us."

After the service Jasmine and I talked to Pastor Luis. We were hoping he would tell us one of his stories, but what he said was even more interesting than a story.

"Are you ready for the missionary conference this week?" Pastor Luis asked. We both nodded. I was going to ask if he knew a missionary story, but Jasmine spoke up first.

"Do you know what I did at the missionary conference last year?" she asked.

"No," said Pastor Luis. "What did you do?"

"Well," Jasmine said, "I listened to what the missionary said all week about people needing to hear about Jesus, so I prayed, and . . ." Jasmine stopped because she was getting shy. I always know when she gets shy because she bites down on her lower lip.

"And what?" Pastor Luis asked.

"And . . . and I felt like I was supposed to go tell them," Jasmine mumbled, and she looked at Pastor Luis like she wasn't sure what he'd think about that. But Pastor Luis just grinned at her and gave her a wink.

"That's the Lord speaking to your heart, Jasmine," Pastor Luis said. "Now what have you done about it?"

"What do you mean?" Jasmine said.

"I mean, have you become a missionary yet?" Pastor Luis had one of those funny twinkles in his eye, the kind he gets when he asks us a tough question.

So I said, "Come on, you're teasing us, Pastor Luis! You know she can't go to the mission field yet. She's just a kid!"

MISSIONARY
SUNDAY
TODAY

"Oh, I know," he said, "She can't be a *going* missionary—at least not yet. But she can be a *waiting* missionary. That's what I am."

"Now I know you're teasing us!" Jasmine said. "You're not a missionary—you're a pastor."

"That's right, I am a pastor," he admitted. "But I'm also a missionary. You see, the Lord spoke to my heart, just like he spoke to yours, Jasmine. And that's when I became a waiting missionary."

Jasmine and I wanted to find out more about what a "waiting" missionary was, but we had to leave. Pastor Luis promised to tell us all about it at the missionary conference.

The missionary who spoke that night was named Mr. Davis. "I'm very glad to be here," he said. "And I can see that missionary work is important to you, because you've decorated the church so nicely. I was also happy to hear that Pastor Luis is planning to go to the mission field."

Jasmine and I looked at each other. Could this be what Pastor Luis meant when he said he was a "waiting" missionary?

After the service, we ran over to Pastor Luis. "Is it true, Pastor? Are you going to another country as a missionary?"

"Yes, Jasmine," Pastor Luis answered. "When I said I'm a waiting missionary, I meant I'm waiting to go on the mission field."

"But Pastor," I said, "I thought it was important for people to hear about Jesus now. What are you waiting for?"

"He's got to prepare himself," Mr. Davis said. He had heard us talking and walked over to join us.

"That's right," Pastor Luis said. "First I went to college, and now I'm working in this church to learn how to do the same kind of work overseas."

"Why are you children so interested in this?" Mr. Davis asked.

When I told him what Jasmine did last year, Mr. Davis' eyes got big. He looked at my sister. "Is this true? Has the Lord spoken to you about becoming a missionary?"

"Y-yes," she said, and she started biting her lip again.

"Why, that's wonderful!" Mr. Davis said, and Jasmine smiled. "Someday, you'll go to the mission field like me and until then, you can be a waiting missionary, like Pastor Luis."

"How do I start?" Jasmine asked.

"There's an important first step," Mr. Davis said. "You must be sure you know Jesus as your Savior."

"I asked Jesus into my heart when I was five," Jasmine said.

"That's good!" Pastor Luis said. "You've got to know the Lord before you can tell others about Him! Now the next thing is to work hard in school so you can go to college."

"I do pretty well in school," Jasmine said. "What else can I do to be a waiting missionary?"

"You can remember to do the things that all Christians are supposed to do," Pastor Luis said. "Things like reading your Bible, praying and telling others about Jesus. And remember to eat all your vegetables!"

"What?" Jasmine and I said together.

"Yes, eat your vegetables," Pastor Luis said. "It's good practice. Missionaries sometimes have to eat some strange foods. If they are picky eaters, they might hurt the feelings of the people they are trying to bring to the Lord. Did you know that Jesus even said so?" And Pastor Luis took his Bible and read Luke 10:8: "When you enter a town and are welcomed, eat what is set before you."

"There are a lot of other things you can do while you're waiting," Mr. Davis added. He walked over to the big globe on the missions display.

"You can write to missionaries and remember to pray for them. You can learn about different countries of the world and what missionaries are doing there. And you can ask God to tell you where He wants you to go and what He wants you to do. There are lots of missionaries who do special jobs, like doctoring, building, computers and music."

"Being a waiting missionary sounds like a lot of hard work," Jasmine said.

"It is," Mr. Davis agreed. "Remember, being a missionary is an important job—just about the most important job there is. The more you do to get ready, the better a missionary you'll be when the time comes to go."

When we got in the car to go home, Jasmine was pretty quiet. She didn't seem so excited about being a missionary anymore. I could tell it was bothering her, because she got mad when I teased her about eating her vegetables.

But later that week at the missionary conference, Mr. Davis spoke about *sacrifice*—that means being willing to give up things to do what God asks you to do.

And on the last night of the missionary conference, when it came time for testimonies, Jasmine stood up.

"I wanted to be a missionary because I thought it would be fun," she said. "But Pastor Luis and Mr. Davis showed me that it's a lot of hard work, too." Then she bit her lip and didn't say anything for a long time.

Finally she added, "But I still want to be a missionary, because I know that's what God wants me to be."

There were a lot of "Amens" from the grownups when she sat down. And I don't think I've ever been prouder of my sister than I was right then. I looked over at Pastor Luis. He had a big grin on his face. I think he was pretty proud of her, too.

ABOUT THE AUTHOR

David E. Fessenden holds the position of editor at Christian Publications in Camp Hill, Pennsylvania, where he manages the publishing schedule for 40 books a year and edits a quarterly missions education journal. He and his wife, Jacque, live in Harrisburg, Pennsylvania, with their sons, Jay and Dan.

Hey Kids!

If you enjoyed *The Waiting Missionary,* why not read other books in the *Missionary—That's Me!* series: *Meet the Missionary, The Missionary Treasure, The Missing Missionary, Missionary—That's Right* and *I Want to Be a Missionary.* And if you enjoy reading stories about missions and missionaries, Christian Publications has two other series available for children: a series of missionary biographies entitled *The Junior Jaffray Collection of Missionary Stories;* and four books of true stories from mission fields around the world—*A Happy Day for Ramona, The Potato Story, The Pink and Green Church* and *Bare, Beautiful Feet.*